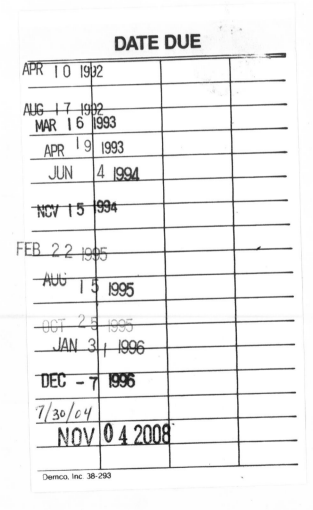

OWLS

ANIMAL FAMILIES

OWLS

Markus Kappeler

Gareth Stevens Children's Books
MILWAUKEE

c1991

ANIMAL FAMILIES

For a free color catalog describing Gareth Stevens' list of high-quality children's books, call 1-800-341-3569 (USA) or 1-800-461-9120 (Canada).

Picture Credits

A.G.E. — 19, 29; Bank Leu — 6; Bruce Coleman — Dermit 25: B. Coates 33: G. D. Plage 37; Hans Dossenbach — 9 (upper right), 22, 32 (right); EMB-Service — 8; Jorg Hess — 23; Jacana — A. Gandolfi 4-5: R. Volot 9 (upper left): J. Ph. Varin 15: Devez NRS 17: F. Gohier 20, 27: R. Konig 30: J. M. Labat 34 (right); Markus Kappeler — 10 (right), 16; Jurg Klages — 1, 21; Felix Labhardt — 11 (upper); Werner Layer — 32 (left); K. H. Lohr — 2, 24 (left); Owl eggs, with the kind permission of the Museum of Natural History, Bern — 11; Okapia — G. Dimijian 26 (right); John O'Neill — 40; Celestino Piatti — 10 (left); Hans Pollin — 18 (upper); Helmut Pum — 18 (lower); Hans Reinhard — 10 (middle), 24 (right), 25 (upper), 26 (left), 27 (left), 31, 35, 36, 38, 39; Manfred Rogl — 4 (left), 12-13, 14, 28; Gunther Synatzschke — 9 (lower), 11 (lower), 34 (left).

Library of Congress Cataloging-in-Publication Data

Kappeler, Markus, 1953-
   [Eulen. English]
   Owls / Markus Kappeler.
      p. cm. — (Animal families)
   Translation of: Eulen.
   Includes bibliographical references and index.
   Summary: Describes the evolution of the owl family and discusses the physical characteristics, habits, and native environment of various members of the species.
   ISBN 0-8368-0687-5
   1. Owls—Juvenile literature. [1. Owls.] I. Title. II. Series: Animal families (Milwaukee, Wis.)
QL696.S8K3613   1991
598'.97—dc20
                                 91-8998

North American edition first published in 1991 by
Gareth Stevens Children's Books
1555 North RiverCenter Drive, Suite 201
Milwaukee, Wisconsin 53212, USA

Series editors: Amy Bauman and Patricia Lantier-Sampon
Editor: Barbara J. Behm
Designer: Sharone Burris
Translated from the German by: Jamie Daniel
Editorial assistants: Scott Enk, Diane Laska, and Andrea J. Schneider

Printed in the United States of America

1 2 3 4 5 6 7 8 9 95 94 93 92 91

Table of Contents

What Is an Owl?

You have probably heard it said that someone is as "wise as an owl." This, just like phrases such as "sly as a fox," "busy as a bee," or "proud as a peacock" is a well known expression. But are these animals really sly, busy, or proud? Are owls really wise?

There has never been any actual proof that this expression — or any of the others — is true. But how, then, did people come up with the idea of attributing wisdom to the owl? There may be several answers to this question. First of all, the owl has certain features that make its face resemble that of a human being. In addition, the owl's physical appearance makes it seem old. In other words, owls have "old men's faces." Because people tend to think of older people as experienced and wise, they attribute these same qualities to the owl.

Owls also have large eyes, with which they quietly and attentively observe things. This gives the impression that they are very intelligent. Then there is the fact that owls can blink their upper eyelids downward and then up again, just as people do. This blinking seems to make owls appear to be very understanding and knowing.

Finally, although owls are nocturnal, people usually come upon them only in the day. When owls are found — often in the rafters of a barn or in some other obscure place — they appear to be deep in thought in the midst of the activity around them. In reality, the owls are simply resting.

Experienced, intelligent, understanding, knowing, deep in thought. At some time, the owl has been associated with all of these

This silver coin with a tawny owl on it was made in ancient Greece. At one time, the coin was simply called an "owl." There were, of course, many such "owls" found in the Greek capital of Athens, where many rich Greeks lived. Even today, the expression "carrying owls to Athens" in Greek means "doing something excessive."

traits. People simply summarize them under the term *wisdom.* Thus, owls haven't become a symbol of wisdom because of their intellectual abilities at all. Rather, people consider them wise because of their appearance and their behavior. Both of these factors can be attributed to their particular life-styles as nocturnal hunters.

Nocturnal Hunters of Small Animals
As the sun sets on the horizon and darkness slowly descends over the forests and fields, a

Ghedruckt Thantwerpen,
Opde Camerpoort-brugghe, inden Schilt van Bafel, by my
Ian van Ghelen de Ionghe, ghefworen Drucker der Con. Ma.
Met Gratie en Priuilegie. 1580

Till Eulenspiegel was a fourteenth-century German folk hero who traveled in search of adventure, playing pranks on the way. The name Eulenspiegel comes from the words euele *(owl) and* spiegel *(mirror), items that became symbolic of the hero. His pranks often proved to be wise teachings (thus the owl), showing people the silliness of their ways (thus the mirror). The symbols and the hero are seen on the book's title page at left.*

Eyes That See in the Dark

The owl's eyes, for example, are extremely sensitive to light. Owls require ten to twenty times less light than humans to be able to see. While humans are blinded by darkness, owls are able to recognize, at a distance, a mouse scurrying through the darkness. Owls achieve such high levels of sensitivity because of the size of their eyes. An owl's eyes take up about a third of the animal's head. If humans had eyes of the same proportions, they would have eyes the size of apples.

In contrast to the human eye, which can roll in all directions, the owl's eyes are rigidly fixed in its skull. If an owl wants to change the direction of its gaze, then, it has to turn its entire head in that direction. This is not a problem for owls, since they have extremely mobile necks with twice as many vertebrae as humans have. Owls are able to rotate their heads about 270 degrees (about three-fourths of a full circle). While sitting peacefully, an owl can turn its head so far to the left that it can see over its right shoulder. This ability has a very practical use. If an owl senses prey somewhere behind it, it doesn't have to turn itself completely around. It can simply turn its head. This movement is much faster and quieter than turning the whole body.

Most birds have eyes on the sides of their heads, but this is not true of the owl. Owls' eyes are set into the front of the head, and both eyes look straight forward. The position of their eyes makes it possible for the nocturnal owls to judge distance. This is extremely important for successful hunting.

great number of small animals become active. Field mice and rabbits emerge from the entrances of the dens in which they have spent the day sleeping. They are hungry and want to go out in search of food under the cover of darkness. At the onset of twilight, the tawny owl, the barn owl, the eagle owl, and most of the other members of the owl family open their round eyes.

Even in darkness, owls can expertly locate and catch their prey. That is how they obtain their nourishment; it is how they survive. Owls can do this because they are well equipped for night hunting. Their sensory organs are extraordinarily sensitive.

Owls are not as colorful as many other birds are. As this photograph shows, most owls' feathers are a combination of white, brown, and black coloring. The coloring of the owl's feathers helps camouflage the bird in its daytime resting place.

Specially Designed Ears

The owl's ears, which are set to the side of the eyes, are also especially sensitive organs. Through tests, biologists have come to believe that owls can hear better than any other living creature on earth. For this reason and in spite of their keen eyesight, most owls rely mainly on their hearing when hunting.

Owls' ears are covered by feathers that form the so-called facial disk. The facial disk is the circle-shaped wreath of feathers around the bird's beak and eyes. These feathers play

In addition to their eyelids, owls have a milky transparent skin that closes over the eye sideways from the base of their bills. This "nodding skin" is especially helpful while owls hunt. Because of it, they are able to keep their eyes moist and clean without having to shut them.

Below: The owl's bill is much larger than you think. It extends under the eye on the side, thus enabling the nocturnal hunters to swallow prey whole.
Bottom: Both of the owl's outer toes are extremely flexible. Known as "revolving toes," they can be pointed forward or backward as needed.

a very important role in the sensitivity of the owl's hearing. They capture the slightest sounds and transmit them to the right and left through a sort of feathered channel to the ears. So instead of capturing sound with outer ear tissues, as do most mammals, an owl captures sound with its facial surfaces.

But owls' ears are sensitive to more than just soft sounds. The ears can also help the bird determine the direction and distance from which a sound has come. The complicated design of the owl's outer ear canals is responsible for this ability. Unlike most birds, which have round ear openings, the owl's ear openings are slit-shaped. In addition, the right ear is located higher on the head than the left ear. This special positioning of its ears also gives the owl information about the sounds it hears.

Another important feature that helps the owl hunt is its feathers. Unlike the feathers of most other birds, the owl's feathers are velvety soft and fluffy. They give the owl a fluffy appearance and protect the bird from the wind as it flies. The feathers also muffle the sounds the owl makes when flying. Any loud flapping noises would warn the owl's

Below left: When an owl opens its eyes in a cartoon, night has fallen. Artists often use the owl to symbolize night, as artist Celestino Piatti has done here. This picture accompanied the Swiss television show "Bedtime Story" for many years.

Below right: Across the world the owl is used to symbolize wisdom. Often it is shown wearing a mortarboard and robe, or sometimes glasses. Occasionally it will be sitting on a book, like the owls shown here.

prey that the owl is coming. In addition, loud flying noises would cover up the soft rustling sounds made by the prey animals. This would make it impossible for the owl to locate prey with its hearing.

Two final features that make the owl a fierce hunter are its claws and its beak. The owl uses its strong legs and sharp-clawed feet to grasp its prey. Then, with its hooked bill, the bird delivers a deadly bite to the prey's neck or back of the head.

They can be seen in the forests of Southeast Asia as well as in the church towers of central European villages. They are found on the smallest islands in the Pacific Ocean and among the mountain peaks in central Asia. They have even been seen circling the ice fields of Greenland and the sun-drenched sand dunes of the Sahara. In all, 140 different types of owls exist throughout the world. A representative from each of the twenty-five species of owls is included in this book.

Considered separately, any one of these specialized parts — the sensitive eyes and ears, the velvet-soft movements, the powerful claws, or the sharp beak — would make a bird a good hunter. Working together, these features make the owl an excellent hunter.

The Adaptable Owl
As masters of night hunting, owls have been able to settle into most habitats of the earth.

Opposite: The eggs of some of the owls covered in this book. (For the purposes of this chart, some of the owl eggs are shown at nine-tenths of their actual size.)

screech owl

common scops owl

Eurasian pygmy owl

burrowing owl

little owl

barn owl

A Guide to *Owls*

hawk owl

tawny owl

long-eared owl

**An owl stands ready to defend its eggs.
Below: A new owlet is already dry.**

northern eagle owl

snowy owl

The Barn Owl

Scientific name: Tyto alba

Length: 13-13.8 inches (33-35 cm)
Weight: 10.6-12.3 ounces (300-350 g)
Wingspan: 33.5-37.4 inches (85-95 cm)

Below: Barn owls perch on a fence. Adult barn owls often show pure white undersides, but light brown or black flecks are common.
Opposite, top: A barn owl carries its catch back to its nest.
Opposite, bottom: Two owls land at a possible nest site.

The barn owl is very different from other owls. It looks different, it has a different call, and, unlike the rest of the owls, it seems to form strong ties to human settlements. These characteristics, as well as strong differences in the barn owl's bone structure, have led biologists to classify the barn owl outside the family of true owls.

In a Family of Its Own
All owls belong to the order Strigiformes. This order is divided into two families: Strigidae and Tytonidae. About 124 kinds of owls, called typical owls, belong to the Strigidae family. Barn owls and bay owls belong to the family Tytonidae.

Even at first glance, the barn owl can be distinguished from other owls because of its heart-shaped facial disk. The barn owl's facial disk is not fixed in one position. Depending on its mood, the barn owl can change the appearance of its face.

The barn owl has long, knock-kneed legs and long, pointed wings. Unlike other owls, the barn owl's wings extend several inches beyond its tail when it is sitting.

An Owl of Many Habitats
The barn owl is a citizen of the world. It can be found on five continents and on four islands. The only areas it does not inhabit are the polar regions. In central Europe, the barn

owl almost always lives near humans. It likes most of all to brood and nest in the clock towers of churches, on the beams of barns, in niches in the walls of ruins, and in other protected sites in buildings.

The barn owl streaks through its hunting territory almost exclusively at night. It preys on small animals up to the size of a rat. Small micelike rodents, called voles, make up almost half of its diet and shrews a quarter of its diet. The remainder consists of house mice, moles, rats, bats, small birds (especially sparrows), frogs, and large insects. It eats the equivalent of approximately four or five mice every day.

During mating season, beginning in February, the male barn owl will present the female with a gift of a dead mouse or other prey. The male will then show the female his nest site and attempt to lure her into it.

In April or May, the female will lay her eggs, known as a clutch. Barn owls usually lay from four to seven eggs, but as many as twelve eggs are possible. The female does not lay all her eggs at once. Instead, she lays the

Young barn owls huddle together, warily watching their surroundings. Some of the owls still wear the fluffy down of very young birds.

eggs in intervals of two or three days. Incubation begins when the first egg has been laid. This means the eggs will hatch at intervals of two or three days. As a result, the chick born from the first egg will be at least two or three days older than the last chick.

If there is enough food available, this difference in age will not be important — all the chicks will survive. If there is a shortage of food, however, the chicks have to compete for the food that their parents bring them. The younger ones will sometimes starve to death. This may seem cruel, but it is the way of nature. When times are tough, two or three strong young birds will have a better chance of survival than five or six weaker ones.

The Bay Owl

Scientific name: Phodilus badius

Length: 10.6-11.4 inches (27-29 cm)
Weight: undetermined
Wingspan: undetermined

think of the bay owl as a transitional form between the two owl families.

The bay owl is at home in the old and vast forests of Southeast Asia, between India and Indonesia. Thanks to its short wings, the bay owl is a particularly agile bird. It is also an excellent hunter in the thick plant growth of its home.

Some owl experts do not consider the bay owl to be a true owl. Because of its particular feathering and skeletal structure, they classify this owl as a member of the barn owl family, Tytonidae. Meanwhile, other experts continue to consider the bay owl as one of the typical owls of the family Strigidae. The most accurate approach to this problem, however, is to

Like most owls, the bay owl does not usually prepare a nest of soft materials to cushion her eggs and young. Instead, the female simply lays her eggs on the bare nest site — the hollow tree or other crevice that the pair has chosen — and incubates them.

Above: *This bay owl's eyes dominate its face.*

The Malay Fish Owl

Scientific name: Ketupa ketupa

Length: 15-17.7 inches (38-45 cm)
Weight: undetermined
Wingspan: undetermined

The Malay fish owl is a fierce-looking bird. With its ear tufts and short wings, it looks somewhat like the northern eagle owl (discussed on pages 18-20). But in spite of similar looks, the two are not close relatives.

The Malay fish owl makes its home in Southeast Asia and on the islands of Sumatra, Borneo, and Java. The preferred habitat of this owl is along quiet forest rivers, in hidden mangrove swamps, and in remote coastal forests. It becomes active in the evening and begins to hunt as the sun sets.

A Resourceful Hunter

Living up to its name, the Malay fish owl is excellent at fishing. It preys on animals that live in or near the water — fish, crabs, shrimp, snakes, birds, rodents, and insect larvae. The Malay fish owl relies on two hunting methods. In the first, which is used only occasionally, the owl wades into shallow water in search of its prey. Moving quietly, the bird surprises a little crab here or an insect larva there. With its quick feet, the bird is upon the prey before it can escape.

In the second method, the bird will wait motionless along the shore on a tree stump or dead branch until it spies a possible victim. Once prey has been sighted, the owl takes flight immediately and is able to catch fish while flying along the water's surface. The Malay fish owl is excellently equipped for catching fish this way. Its claws have razor-sharp underside edges, and the soles of its feet are equipped with sharp scales. Even for slippery and wriggling prey, there is no escape from these feet. Grasping the fish in its claws, the bird can catch its prey without interrupting its flight.

The Malay fish owl is a strong, clever hunter. Despite its powerful beak, this owl relies almost entirely on its claws for hunting.

Pel's Fishing Owl

Scientific name: Scotopelia peli

Length: 20-24 inches (51-61 cm)
Weight: 4.4-5.1 pounds (2-2.3 kg)
Wingspan: 4.9 feet (1.5 m)

A large round head with dark eyes and shaggy feathers are characteristic of Pel's fishing owl. With a body length of up to 24 inches (61 cm) and a wingspan of 59 inches (1.5 m), it is among the largest owls in the world. Pel's fishing owl can be found in Africa south of the Sahara Desert.

Like the Malay fish owl, Pel's fishing owl lives by catching fish and uses some of the same methods. It usually leaves its resting place as the sun sets to begin a night of fishing. Like the Malay fish owl, Pel's fishing owl is excellently equipped for catching fish with its giant, sharp-edged claws and the barbed scales on its feet and legs.

Pel's fishing owl devours between 3.5 and 10.6 ounces (100-300 g) of fish per day. But fishing owls have occasionally been spotted carrying perch weighing 2 pounds (0.9 kg). This round-headed night bird loves to supplement its diet with frogs, shrimp, small mammals, and even young crocodiles.

Pel's fishing owls live in pairs throughout the year in certain hunting territories where they won't tolerate the presence of others of their own kind. Abandoned eagles' nests and spacious hollow trees serve as their brood nests. There the female will lay from two to four eggs during the dry season. During this season, the water level in the rivers is low and the water flows slowly. This makes it relatively easy for owls to spot prey in the water. Thus, the parents have an easier time filling the mouths of their never-satisfied young.

The young birds hatch after an incubation period of five weeks. Ten weeks later, they can leave the nest and fly, but they remain dependent on their parents for about four more months. By then, they have mastered the art of fishing and can go out on their own.

Pel's fishing owl and the Malay fish owl are thought to have evolved from the same ancestors. If so, the two species must have split off from each other long ago, because they do not look alike.

The Northern Eagle Owl

Scientific name: Bubo bubo

Length: 23.6-28 inches (60-71 cm)
Weight: 4.4-7 pounds (2-3.2 kg)
Wingspan: 4.9-5.9 feet (1.5-1.8 m)

Below: At four weeks of age, young northern eagle owls will raise their wings and practice attacks against the remains of prey lying nearby.
Bottom: A northern eagle owl exhibits its threatening stance. These feisty birds have lived as long as sixty-eight years in captivity.
Opposite: The world's largest owl has a wingspan that can equal the height of an adult human being.

With a wingspan of nearly 6 feet (1.8 m), the northern eagle owl is the world's largest owl. It lags just behind the golden eagle, whose wingspan measures from 6.6 to 7.5 feet (2-2.3 m). The northern eagle owl is often called "the king of the night." This honor, however, belongs only to the female owl. While it is difficult to tell males from females in most owl species, the female northern eagle owl is noticeably larger than the male.

The northern eagle owl makes its home in Europe, Asia, and North Africa. Within this broad territorial range, it doesn't limit itself to one type of landscape or climate. It makes its home in valleys, high mountains, thick forests, and on stark plains. This owl has even been seen in desert terrain. To survive in an area, the owl needs only an adequate supply of prey and plenty of places for daytime hideaways and nesting.

shelter of an overhanging rock or among branches close to the trunk of a tree. If surprised by an enemy, such as a fox or a hawk, this owl takes a threatening stance. With eyes wide open, feathers raised, and wings fanned out and turned forward, the northern eagle owl will lean forward, screeching and snapping its beak. This fear-

A Flexible Bird

The northern eagle owl is also quite flexible about what it will eat. With clawed feet that spread as wide as a human hand, it can grab almost anything that crosses its path, from beetles, frogs, and shrews to fish and snakes. It also commonly preys on woodchucks, jack-rabbits, and herons, but even weasels, martens, wildcats, buzzards, and falcons are not safe from this powerful bird.

Typically, the northern eagle owl is active only at night. During the day, it hides in the

inspiring sight seldom fails. As the enemy stands stunned, the owl makes its escape.

In February, the call of the male northern eagle owl pierces the chilly night. With his "buoh — buoh — buoh" the male stakes his territory. At the same time, he is calling to his mate that it is once again time to produce offspring. The female responds to the male's call with a higher, softer, two-syllable "hu — hu." These duets are often accompanied by a guttural twittering, as well as clucking and cawing sounds.

Between mid-March and mid-April, the female will lay two, three, or even four eggs. She lays the eggs at intervals of two to four days in niches and hollows in the rocky crags. Then she will incubate the eggs for a full five weeks before the first one hatches.

At three weeks of age, the birds begin to actively walk about the nest. At seven weeks,

and pheasants that people wanted as food. This owl was therefore heavily hunted by people for centuries and is now extinct in many areas of Europe.

Today, only about eighty brood pairs remain in Switzerland, about two hundred live in Austria, and perhaps three hundred can still be found in Germany. To help the

they leave the nest on foot and run through the underbrush in search of adventure, well guarded by their parents. They are finally able to fly at ten weeks and can accompany their parents on hunting trips. By autumn, they will be able to hunt for themselves, at which point they will leave their parents.

The Northern Eagle Owl's Future
The northern eagle owl was once considered a pest by some people because the owl occasionally made off with rabbits, partridges,

northern eagle owl, conservationists have raised several thousand of these birds in captivity and then set them free. The success rate of this effort has been moderate, since the owl faces many dangers. In addition to its enemies, this owl must also deal with disturbances at its nesting sites created by all types of human activity.

The American great horned owl (above) and the Malay eagle owl (right) are closely related to the northern eagle owl (shown on pages 18-19).

The Snowy Owl

Scientific name: Nyctea scandiaca

Length: 20.9-26 inches (53-66 cm)
Weight: 3.3-5.3 pounds (1.5-2.4 kg)
Wingspan: about 5 feet (1.5 m)

The snowy owl is almost as big as the northern eagle owl and is among the giants of the owl family. This owl can be found in Europe, Asia, and North America. On all three continents, this owl's favorite habitat is the Arctic tundra. It prefers the treeless landscape of the far north, which is covered with snow throughout most of the year.

The snowy owl has adapted well to the raw climate of its home. Its black and white feathers are the longest and thickest of any owl's. This covering keeps the snowy owl warm in even the most bitter cold. It also blends well with the snow and rocks, perfectly camouflaging the bird. This camouflage protects the snowy owl from enemies and helps it approach its prey unnoticed.

As further protection from the cold, the snowy owl's hooked bill is encased in a "beard" of feather bristles and its feet are feather-covered to the tips of its toes. In addition, the snowy owl stores body fat. It is the only type of owl able to do so. It can pack away almost two pounds (900 g) of fat over a summer. This enables the owl to easily withstand the long, hard winter, when snow and thick fog often make hunting impossible.

The Owl and the Lemming
This owl can overpower almost every other animal in its snowy home. Its prey includes over fifty types of mammals, from the shrew to the Arctic fox, and ninety types of birds, from the sparrow to the gray goose. However, rodents called lemmings make up over three-quarters of the snowy owl's diet.

The life of the snowy owl is closely linked with that of this rodent. For example, snowy owls don't brood on mountaintops, although they are suited to the climate, because lemmings do not live there. In fact, the availability of lemmings determines the size of the snowy owl's clutch. In good years, when lemmings are abundant, the female owl may lay up to eleven eggs. In years when lemmings are particularly scarce, she may lay only three or four eggs or none at all. Also, when lemmings die off in an area (as happens naturally every few years), many snowy owls must move to avoid starvation. When this happens, young owls with less hunting experience flee south. In Europe, they sometimes end up as far south as Austria, in Asia as far as India, and in North America as far as Texas.

In contrast to most other types of owls, male and female snowy owls look quite different. The male (opposite) wears a feather coat that is almost completely white. The feathers of the female (above left) are covered with dark speckles.

The Common Scops Owl

Scientific name: Otus scops

Length: 7.5-7.9 inches (19-20 cm)
Weight: 2.8-3.4 ounces (80-95 g)
Wingspan: 19.7-23.6 inches (50-60 cm)

The flammulated scops owl (below right), the white-fronted scops owl (opposite top), and the common screech owl (opposite bottom) are related to the common scops owl (below left).

The common scops owl has small ear feathers. Frequently, these feathers lie so flat against the owl's head that they can't be seen at all. The hornlike feathers are only clearly recognizable when the little owl is frightened. Then, the feathers rise up stiffly on its head.

Unlike other owls, the common scops owl is a migrator. In the summer, it inhabits the territories around the Mediterranean Sea and throughout central Asia. Here the female will brood and raise her young. In autumn she will fly south and spend the winter on the African savannas south of the Sahara Desert.

The common scops owls of Siberia have the longest distance to cover. They must travel for about two months and cover a total of almost 5,000 miles (8,000 km). This is quite an achievement for such a small owl.

The migratory behavior of the common scops owl can be linked with the bird's diet. Large insects — particularly grasshoppers — are its favorite prey. Because of their loud chirping, grasshoppers are also easy to catch. Fortunately, these and other insects are plentiful during the warm season, when the owl has young to feed. In autumn, however,

as the weather grows cooler, insects become harder to find. This forces the common scops owl to migrate to warmer regions, where food will again be plentiful.

Unfortunately, the long trip is dangerous for the common scops owl. In many places, these birds are considered a delicacy. As they fly over Europe, the Mediterranean islands, and North Africa, many of the little owls are captured in nets or shot.

The White-faced Owl

Scientific name: Ptilopsis leucotis

Length: 7.5-9.4 inches (19-24 cm)
Weight: undetermined
Wingspan: undetermined

The white-faced owl is found in Africa. It lives primarily south of the Sahara Desert in the savannas. After sunset, it hunts for grasshoppers and any other buzzing and chirping insects.

Like all owls, the white-faced owl is a very vocal bird. Frequent calling is important to these night birds so that the males and females or parents and young can find each other in the dark. What is unusual, though, is that white-faced owls speak two different languages within their wide territorial range. The night call of the white-faced owls of western Africa is a clear "kukukuooo." The white-faced owls in southern Africa, however, make a rattling "vrrrrrrrrooo" call.

The Crested Owl

Scientific name: Lophostrix cristata

Length: 15.7-16.9 inches (40-43 cm)
Weight: undetermined
Wingspan: undetermined

With its long, white crests of feathers hanging over its eyes, the crested owl cannot be mistaken for any other type of owl. This bird makes its home in the warm and humid ancient forests of Central and South America.

Little is known about the life-style of the elusive crested owl in the wild. Like most owls, it seems to exist on a diet as varied as possible. It will eat almost anything that creeps or flies through its territory, including rodents, shrimp, frogs, lizards, grasshoppers, moths, bats, and even smaller birds.

Above left: White-faced owls nest in trees in the African savanna.
Above: The crested owl has a distinct face.

The Spectacled Owl

Scientific name: Pulsatrix perspicillata

Length: 16.9-18.1 inches (43-46 cm)
Weight: 1.3-2.2 pounds (600 g-1 kg)
Wingspan: undetermined

The spectacled owl gets its name from the striking wreathlike pattern of its facial disk. This large owl makes its home in the rain forests and mangrove swamps of Central and South America.

The most frequent sound made by the spectacled owl is a rattling series of short individual calls that sound like the hammering of a woodpecker. The native people of Brazil call this owl the "knocking bird." They refer to the young of the spectacled owl as "white birds" because of their stark white coloring. Unlike their parents, young spectacled owls wear a snow white coat of feathers. Only their faces and wings are tinted a dark brown.

The Mottled Owl

Scientific name: Ciccaba virgata

Length: 11.8-14.2 inches (30-36 cm)
Weight: 6.3-8.8 ounces (180-250 g)
Wingspan: undetermined

The mottled owl's territorial range extends from Mexico south to Argentina. This middle-sized night predator is mottled on top — in other words, its otherwise grayish brown coat of feathers is covered in that area with many bright spots.

The mottled owl does not prefer any particular kind of habitat. It is as happy living in shadowy woods at sea level as in the straw thickets along mountain inclines, in open grasslands with isolated wooded areas, or on mountainous coffee plantations that have been cultivated by people.

Above left and right: Both the spectacled owl and the mottled owl have bold facial markings that call attention to their eyes.

The Tawny Owl

Scientific name: Strix aluco

Length: 15-16.5 inches (38-42 cm)
Weight: 1-1.3 pounds (450-600 g)
Wingspan: 35.4-39.4 inches (90-100 cm)

u-vitt" as a command to "come with." They believed that this was the "bird of death" calling them to their graves. The call of the tawny owl actually has more to do with life than with death. As a mating call, it is used to bring a pair of owls together.

Young tawny owls usually come into the world in a hollow tree trunk. Like many other

The tawny owl can be found in Europe, northern Africa, and in select areas of Asia. In central Europe, it is by far the most common type of owl. It can be spotted in practically any large wooded area. The tawny owl is not especially shy around people and has been known to brood in parking structures in the middle of very populated locations.

The ringing "huu-hu-huuuu" call of the male tawny owl can often be heard on clear spring nights. The female will answer with a piercing "ke-u-vitt." In the past, people were very afraid of these calls. They heard the "ke-

newborn owls, they leave the nest well before they can fly properly. Because of this, they frequently land on the ground or in a tangle of underbrush. When people come upon a helpless, young owl, they are tempted to "rescue" it and take it home. It is best to leave the tiny bird alone. Parent birds are never far away, and owls, especially, are known to be fiercely defensive of their young.

Above: A young tawny owl ventures from the nest.
Opposite: An adult tawny owl readies its powerful clawed feet for a landing.

The Striped Owl

Scientific name: Rhinoptynx clamator

Length: 12.2-15 inches (31-38 cm)
Weight: 10.6-14.1 ounces (300-400 g)
Wingspan: undetermined

The striped owl lives mainly on small mammals.

In some languages, the striped owl is called the "shrieking owl" because of its shrill cry. Its territorial range extends from Mexico in the north to Argentina in the south. In this huge area, this long-eared tropical bird lives in any type of forest, including rain forests, monsoon forests, and swamp forests. With short, rounded wings and a long tail, it is well equipped for hunting in these environments. It can fly with ease through the narrowest spaces and completely surprise its prey.

The Long-eared Owl

Scientific name: Asio otus

Length: 13.8-14.6 inches (35-37 cm)
Weight: 9.5-12.3 ounces (270-350 g)
Wingspan: 35.4-39.4 inches (90-100 cm)

The long-eared owl is at home in broad sections of Europe, Asia, northern Africa, and North America. Its favorite habitats are areas bordering thick pine forests. This owl usually spends the day perched on a branch in a dark, protected part of a pine tree. There it can sleep peacefully without being disturbed. At night, the owl will venture out into nearby fields and meadows to search for prey. Unlike many other owls, the long-eared owl has a very specific diet. Rodents called voles make up from 80 to 100 percent of its intake. Over a year, it may eat as many as one thousand of these little rodents. This makes the long-eared owl one of the most efficient "mousers" in the world.

Like the striped owl, the white-faced owl, the northern eagle owl, and many other types of owls, the long-eared owl has feathery "ear" tufts. Owl experts have not yet determined what purpose these feathers serve. Some experts believe that they are part of the owl's sensory equipment. Because these mobile and highly sensitive tufts extend directly from the facial disk, they may help capture sound. Other experts believe that the tufts are merely for decoration or help give the owl a frightening appearance.

Opposite: A fierce-looking face can be an advantage for an owl. Many owls have big, bold-colored eyes surrounded by striking markings that frighten attackers. The ear tufts of the striped owl and the long-eared owl add to that appearance.

The Northern Hawk Owl

Scientific name: Surnia ulula

Length: 14.2-16.1 inches (36-41 cm)
Weight: 8.1-12.3 ounces (230-350 g)
Wingspan: 27.6-31.5 inches (70-80 cm)

The northern hawk owl is at home in the northernmost pine forests of Europe, Asia, and North America. There it can be observed, unlike most other owls, hunting by day. Often, this owl hunts in the early morning or early evening, but it has been seen at midday.

The northern hawk owl's name comes from the fact that it is often mistaken for a hawk. The owl's long tail, tapered wings, and brown-and-white-banded belly are the basis for this comparison. But this owl also hunts for prey in much the same way as a hawk hunts. Like the hawk, the owl will hover in the air until it spots prey and then suddenly swoop upon it. Even the northern hawk owl's call is similar to that of a hawk.

The Boobook Owl

Scientific name: Ninox novaeseelandiae

Length: 11-14.2 inches (28-36 cm)
Weight: undetermined
Wingspan: undetermined

The medium-sized boobook owl makes its home in southern locations such as Australia, as well as the islands of New Zealand and New Guinea. Its clear, two-syllable call — "boo-book" — gives the boobook owl its name.

The boobook owl uses hollows in old trees as brooding places. Here, young owls, who initially wear a coat of white down and look like restless balls of cotton, are well protected from enemies and can grow up in safety.

Opposite: A close-up of a Papuan hawk owl.
Below left: Like hawks, the northern hawk owl often uses a high perch to watch for prey. Voles are the favorite catch of this bird.
Below: By the time it is an adult, the boobook owl wears a spotted coat.

The Papuan Hawk Owl

Scientific name: Uroglaux dimorpha

Length: 11.8-13 inches (30-33 cm)
Weight: undetermined
Wingspan: undetermined

The Papuan hawk owl inhabits the vast tropical rain forests of New Guinea, the second largest island in the world. Two things are unusual about this dark owl with the big, yellow-gold eyes. First, it has an especially long tail that makes up almost half of its total length. Second, it has markedly short wings that are rounded off on the outside edges. These two traits are distinguishing characteristics of all forest owls, who must be able to navigate narrow passages and sharp curves while flying after prey through a maze of plant growth. Its body structure makes the Papuan hawk owl one of the great masters of hunting in the forest.

Not many details are known about the life-style of the Papuan hawk owl in the wild. Its remote island location has made it difficult for scientists to study it in detail.

The Fearful Owl

Scientific name: Nesasio solomonensis

Length: 11-15 inches (28-38 cm)
Weight: undetermined
Wingspan: undetermined

The fearful owl (not pictured) is found exclusively on the Solomon Islands in the Pacific Ocean. Within this remote group of islands, the bird lives only on the three islands of Bougainville, Choiseul, and Santa Isabel. Because of its limited range, this owl is one of the rarest types of owls in the world.

The fearful owl has a beautiful white face with expressive yellow eyes. The rest of its feathered body is yellow with dark brown spots. Not much is known about the life-style of this owl, as it was not discovered until the twentieth century. However, its extremely powerful bill and clawed feet indicate that its diet probably consists of medium-sized prey.

The Jamaican Owl

Scientific name: Pseudoscops grammicus

Length: 11-12.6 inches (28-32 cm)
Weight: undetermined
Wingspan: undetermined

The Jamaican owl (not pictured) is another island dweller. It lives only on Jamaica, a small island in the Caribbean Sea. It is another extremely rare owl.

This owl has bright brown feathers with darker stripes and flecks, yellow eyes, and small, feathered ears. It lives in wooded areas as well as on bush-covered land where it hunts mainly at night for small animals. As it hunts, this owl makes calls of "vow" and a trembling "huuuuuh."

The Little Owl

Scientific name: Athene noctua

Length: 7.9-8.7 inches (20-22 cm)
Weight: 5.6-7 ounces (160-200 g)
Wingspan: 21.7-23.6 inches (55-60 cm)

Below left and right: A female little owl may easily have as many as five or six owlets each mating season. The larger the brood, the greater the demand on the adult birds who must feed the young owls.
Opposite: A pair of little owls perches among the tree branches. As adults, the owls have coats flecked with white.

The owl known as the little owl can be found in Europe, northern Africa, and central Asia. In central Europe, it prefers to live in a variety of habitats, such as fields, woods, and meadows with fruit trees and hedges. Here the little owl finds many resting places and hollows for nesting, as well as a plentiful and varied supply of food.

The little owl often begins to hunt before sundown. This is especially true in spring, when its newly hatched offspring never stop begging for food. It is often possible to spot the little owl in the woods at this time of year. Usually, this owl is not overly excited when encountering people. In fact, little owls sometimes nest in towns, just as the tawny owl does.

Wherever the little owl perches, it leaves behind small pellets. These are the remains of whatever the bird has eaten a few hours before. The pellets are regurgitated in the form of round, furry balls. Like all owls, the little owl gulps down its prey all in one piece. Parts that the bird cannot digest, such as bones, hair, feathers, and insect shells, are compressed together in the bird's stomach and then brought up again. The little owl will open its bill wide, jump from one foot to the other, close its eyes tight, choke, and tremble until finally ridding itself of the thick pellet. The pellets are usually 1.2 to 1.6 inches (3-4 cm) long and 0.6 inch (1.5 cm) across.

Scientists examine the pellets and can determine the little owl's diet. Observation of 2,500 little-owl pellets revealed that it eats a variety of food — crickets, moths, beetles, snails, earthworms, frogs, lizards, sparrows, blackbirds, and all sorts of mice. The fact that rats and even weasels also fall victim to the little owl, who weighs 7 ounces (200 g) at the most, indicates that this owl is an accomplished hunter.

Unfortunately, the little owl has grown rare in several parts of Europe. This is mainly because of modern agricultural practices, which have eliminated high-stemmed fruit trees, hedges, and wooded fields. Without places in which to brood, the little owl will not survive. In recent years, conservationists have tried to help the little owl by introducing artificial nesting sites. If the owl can adapt to this new housing, it will have a greater chance of survival.

The Burrowing Owl

Scientific name: Speotyto cunicularia

Length: 9-10.6 inches (23-27 cm)
Weight: undetermined
Wingspan: undetermined

The burrowing owl's habitat has been reduced as grasslands have been converted into cropland.

The burrowing owl makes its home on the wide prairies of North America and the grasslands, called pampas or llanos, of South America. This stiff-legged owl is called the burrowing owl because of the burrows it uses for its nest. The owl does not generally dig these hollows itself, however. Rather, it moves into burrows that have been abandoned by prairie dogs, armadillos, and other animals.

Like other owls, the burrowing owl has different calls for different situations. One of this owl's calls sounds much like the warning rattle of a rattlesnake. The owl uses this call to frighten enemies, such as polecats, away from its home. Even young burrowing owls know this effective defense and thus remain undisturbed in their burrows.

The Elf Owl

Scientific name: Micrathene whitneyi

Length: 5.1-5.5 inches (13-14 cm)
Weight: undetermined
Wingspan: 13.4 inches (34 cm)

Along with the long-whiskered owl, the elf owl is one of the smallest owls in the world. When this tiny owl flies about after the sun sets, it looks more like a large moth than a bird.

The elf owl inhabits the Sierra Madre mountain range in Mexico as well as other desert areas of North America. It also can be found in woods near these deserts. Natural hollows in old oak or maple trees sometimes serve as nests for the elf owl. However, this owl much prefers abandoned woodpecker holes in tall cacti. The bird is well protected in this home because not many predators want to climb these prickly plants. The cactus also protects the birds from the harsh desert climate. By day, it keeps the owl's nest cool even in the blistering midday heat. Later, still warm from the day's heat, the cactus will keep the owls warm long after the desert temperature has dropped for the night.

In April or May, the female elf owl lays two to five eggs at intervals of about two days. After three weeks, the eggs hatch. Like all owlets, young elf owls come into the world with closed eyes. They also wear white, downy coats and look like balls of wool. Each day, as it grows dark, the owlets begin to beg for food, squawking loudly. This "begging call" keeps the parent owls hunting through the night. The adults return to the nest every five to ten minutes carrying beetles, moths, caterpillars, or other insects.

Opposite: Insects and their larvae are the elf owl's main prey. But this bird has learned to make use of any food source its environment provides and will also eat lizards and scorpions.

Tengmalm's Owl

Scientific name: Aegolius funereus

Length: 9.1-9.8 inches (23-25 cm)
Weight: 4.6-6 ounces (130-170 g)
Wingspan: 21.7-23.6 inches (55-60 cm)

Three young Tengmalm's owls perch on a branch near their nest and wait for their parents' return. The Tengmalm's owl's nesting site must provide cover that hides the nest from predators flying overhead but allows the owl to watch for predators coming from below.

Tengmalm's owl, also known as the boreal owl, can be found in all of the cooler regions of the Northern Hemisphere. This owl is well adapted to this chilly environment, since it has an especially thick coat of feathers. Also, like the snowy owl, this owl's feet are covered with soft feathers down to the claws.

Tengmalm's owl prefers to live in old, dark pine forests. There it chooses an unoccupied woodpecker hole for a brooding nest. In its hollow, the owl must stay alert for predators, which include such animals as the fierce pine marten and even larger owls.

After mid-April, the female lays four to seven eggs. Like many owls, the coffee brown Tengmalm's owlets will leave the nest before they can fly. Then they will sit on nearby branches and wait for their parents to bring food to them. Soon enough, they will learn to capture their own prey.

The Eurasian Pygmy Owl

Scientific name: Glaucidium passerinum

Length: 6.3-7.1 inches (16-18 cm)
Weight: 1.8-2.6 ounces (50-75 g)
Wingspan: 13.8-15.8 inches (35-40 cm)

The tiny Eurasian pygmy owl is only slightly larger than a sparrow. It can be found from Scandinavia and central Europe to as far east as Manchuria. This bird is closely related to the northern pygmy owl, which is about the same size, and is found throughout much of North and Central America.

In its vast territory, the Eurasian pygmy owl lives in large, high-stemmed woods. Most often it nests in abandoned woodpecker holes. There this owl is sometimes heard singing loudly from the tops of tall trees. With this call, the owl warns any other owls that might be in the area that the territory is occupied. The song consists of increasingly higher scales with six to eight "duh" calls and is especially common in the fall.

The Eurasian pygmy owl is active primarily in the early morning hours, when it haunts nearby clearings in search of prey. This owl is a quick, attentive hunter who will attack birds such as titmice and finches up to its own size, as well as mice of all sorts and sizes. In winter, the Eurasian pygmy owl carefully sets aside an emergency supply of food in old woodpecker holes for days when fog or snow make it impossible to hunt. Sometimes this owl's store will include as many as thirty small birds. Little wonder, then, that the Eurasian pygmy owl is not liked by other birds of the forest. If they discover the owl anywhere during the day, they will screech and twitter loudly until the owl moves on.

The Eurasian pygmy owl scans its territory from a high perch.

An Encouraging Discovery

The long-whiskered owlet (*Xenoglaux loweryi*) is about 5.1 to 5.5 inches (13-14 cm) long and weighs 1.6 to 1.8 ounces (45-50 g). This owl is known for the long, hairlike feathers that grow on its face and stand out in all directions.

But the long-whiskered owlet is a unique bird for a different reason. It was first discovered in 1976, in the foggy forests of the Rio Mayo valley in Peru. Today, when so many animals are either threatened with extinction or already extinct, the long-whiskered owlet is an inspiring new discovery. It reminds people that the earth still has its quiet, undisturbed corners where animals and plants can live in peace. The greatest care must be taken to preserve these natural paradises.

APPENDIX TO ANIMAL FAMILIES

OWLS

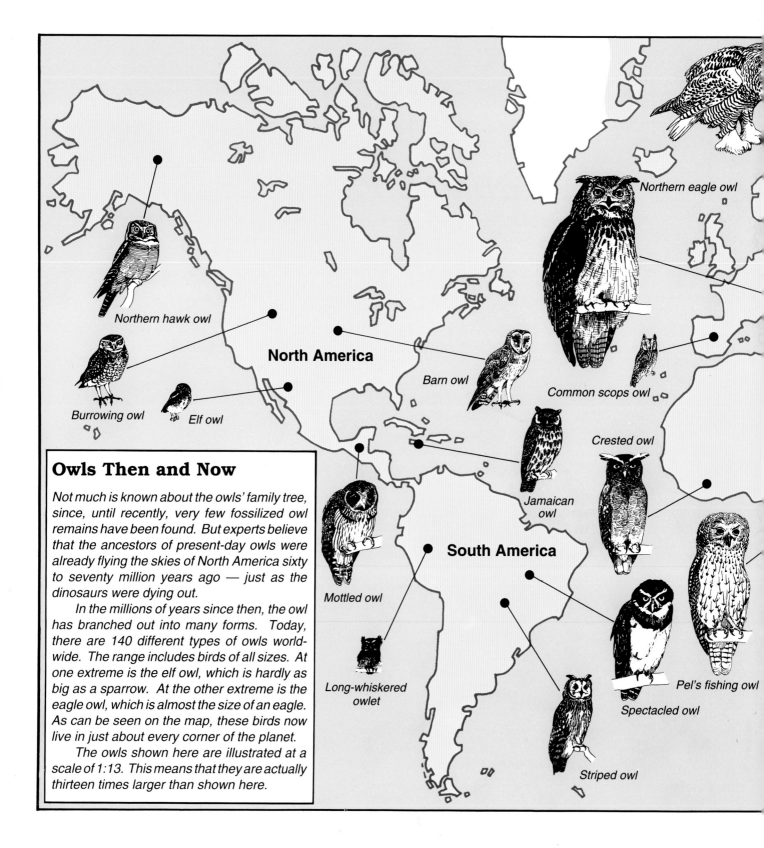

Northern eagle owl

Northern hawk owl

North America

Barn owl

Common scops owl

Burrowing owl

Elf owl

Crested owl

Jamaican owl

Owls Then and Now

Not much is known about the owls' family tree, since, until recently, very few fossilized owl remains have been found. But experts believe that the ancestors of present-day owls were already flying the skies of North America sixty to seventy million years ago — just as the dinosaurs were dying out.

In the millions of years since then, the owl has branched out into many forms. Today, there are 140 different types of owls worldwide. The range includes birds of all sizes. At one extreme is the elf owl, which is hardly as big as a sparrow. At the other extreme is the eagle owl, which is almost the size of an eagle. As can be seen on the map, these birds now live in just about every corner of the planet.

The owls shown here are illustrated at a scale of 1:13. This means that they are actually thirteen times larger than shown here.

South America

Mottled owl

Long-whiskered owlet

Spectacled owl

Pel's fishing owl

Striped owl

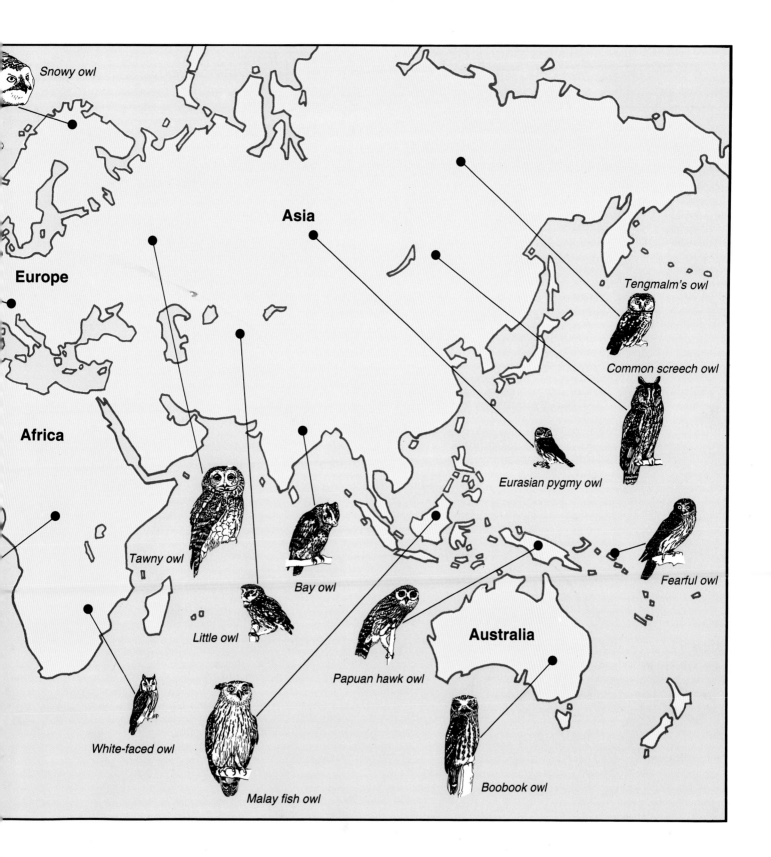

Snowy owl

Asia

Europe

Africa

Tengmalm's owl

Common screech owl

Eurasian pygmy owl

Tawny owl

Bay owl

Fearful owl

Little owl

Papuan hawk owl

Australia

White-faced owl

Malay fish owl

Boobook owl

43

ABOUT THESE BOOKS

Although this series is called "Animal Families," these books aren't just about fathers, mothers, and young. They also discuss the scientific definition of *family*, which is a division of biological classification and includes many animals.

Biological classification is a method that scientists use to identify and organize living things. Using this system, scientists place animals and plants into larger groups that share similar characteristics. Characteristics are physical features, natural habits, ancestral backgrounds, or any other qualities that make one organism either like or different from another.

The method used today for biological classification was introduced in 1753 by a Swedish botanist-naturalist named Carolus Linnaeus. Although many scientists tried to find ways to classify the world's plants and animals, Linnaeus's system seemed to be the only useful choice. Charles Darwin, a famous British naturalist, referred to Linnaeus's system in his theory of evolution, which was published in his book *On the Origin of Species* in 1859. Linnaeus's classification system, shown below, includes seven major categories, or groups. These are: kingdom, phylum, class, order, family, genus, and species.

An easy way to remember the divisions and their order is to memorize this sentence: "Ken Put Cake On Frank's Good Shirt." The first letter of each word in this sentence gives you the first letter of a division. (The *K* in *Ken*, for example, stands for *kingdom*.) The order of the words in the sentence suggests the order of the divisions from largest to smallest. The kingdom is the largest of these divisions; the species is the smallest. The larger the division, the more types of animals or plants it contains. For example, the animal kingdom, called Animalia, contains everything from worms to whales. Smaller divisions, such as the family, have fewer members that share more characteristics. For example, members of the bear family, Ursidae, include the polar bear, the brown bear, and many others.

In the following chart, the lion species is followed through all seven categories. As the categories expand to include more and more members, remember that only a few examples are pictured here. Each division has many more members.

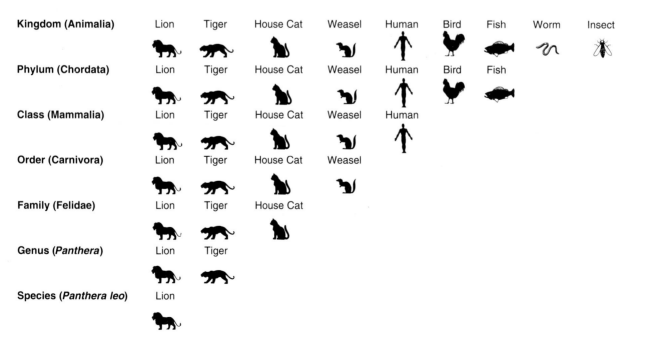

	Lion	Tiger	House Cat	Weasel	Human	Bird	Fish	Worm	Insect
Kingdom (Animalia)	Lion	Tiger	House Cat	Weasel	Human	Bird	Fish	Worm	Insect
Phylum (Chordata)	Lion	Tiger	House Cat	Weasel	Human	Bird	Fish		
Class (Mammalia)	Lion	Tiger	House Cat	Weasel	Human				
Order (Carnivora)	Lion	Tiger	House Cat	Weasel					
Family (Felidae)	Lion	Tiger	House Cat						
Genus (*Panthera*)	Lion	Tiger							
Species (*Panthera leo*)	Lion								

SCIENTIFIC NAMES OF THE ANIMALS IN THIS BOOK

Animals have different names in every language. For this reason, researchers the world over use the same scientific names, which usually stem from ancient Greek or Latin. Most animals are classified by two names. One is the genus name; the other is the name of the species to which they belong. Additional names indicate further subgroupings. Here is a list of the animals included in *Owls*.

Barn owl	*Tyto alba*
Bay owl	*Phodilus badius*
Boobook owl	*Ninox novaeseelandiae*
Burrowing owl	*Speotyto cunicularia*
Common scops owl	*Otus scops*
Common screech owl	*Otus asio*
Crested owl	*Lophostrix cristata*
Elf owl	*Micrathene whitneyi*
Eurasian pygmy owl	*Glaucidium passerinum*
Fearful owl	*Nesasio solomonensis*
Jamaican owl	*Pseudoscops grammicus*
Little owl	*Athene noctua*
Long-eared owl	*Asio otus*
Long-whiskered owlet	*Xenoglaux loweryi*
Malay fish owl	*Ketupa ketupa*
Mottled owl	*Ciccaba virgata*
Northern eagle owl	*Bubo bubo*
Northern hawk owl	*Surnia ulula*
Papuan hawk owl	*Uroglaux dimorpha*
Pel's fishing owl	*Scotopelia peli*
Snowy owl	*Nyctea scandiaca*
Spectacled owl	*Pulsatrix perspicillata*
Striped owl	*Rhinoptynx clamator*
Tawny owl	*Strix aluco*
Tengmalm's owl	*Aegolius funereus*
White-faced owl	*Ptilopsis leucotis*

GLOSSARY

brooding
The act of a parent bird sitting on or over its young to keep them warm.

camouflage
To conceal or hide by disguise. The color and markings of many animals, including owls, camouflage them by helping them blend into their natural surroundings.

carnivore
A predominantly meat-eating animal.

class
The third of seven divisions in the biological classification system proposed by the Swedish botanist-naturalist Carolus Linnaeus. The class is the main subdivision of the phylum. Owls and all other birds belong to the class known as Aves.

climate
The type of weather (including temperature, precipitation, and wind) that prevails in an area.

clutch
A number of eggs produced at one time.

environment
The conditions, circumstances, and influences affecting the development of an animal or group of animals.

evolution
The gradual process of change that occurs in any organism and its descendants over a long period of time. Organisms evolve in order to survive the changes that can occur in climate, food supply, air quality, and other such factors.

extinction
The end or destruction of a specific type of living organism (plant or animal).

facial disk
The circle-shaped wreath of seemingly fixed feathers around an owl's beak and eyes. The facial disk plays a role in the owl's sensitive hearing by receiving sounds and transmitting them to the owl's eardrums.

family
The fifth of seven divisions in the biological classification system proposed by the Swedish botanist-naturalist Carolus Linnaeus. The family is the main subdivision

of the order and contains one or more genera. Owls belong to one of two families: Tytonidae or Strigidae.

genus (plural: **genera**)
The sixth of seven divisions in the biological classification system proposed by botanist-naturalist Carolus Linnaeus. A genus is the main subdivision of a family and includes one or more species.

gestation period
The number of days from actual conception to the birth of an animal. Gestation periods vary greatly for different types of animals.

habitat
The area or type of environment in which an animal normally lives or occurs.

herbivore
An animal whose diet consists mainly of plants.

immobile
Unable to move. An owl's eyes are rigidly fixed in its skull and are therefore completely immobile.

kingdom
The first of seven divisions in the biological classification system proposed by botanist-naturalist Carolus Linnaeus. Owls, like all other animals (including human beings), belong to the kingdom Animalia.

migrator
An animal that moves from one region or climate to another. Migrating often takes place from season to season and is done for mating or feeding purposes.

naturalist
A person who studies and observes plants and animals in their natural settings.

nocturnal
Active at night and usually asleep during the day. Most owls are nocturnal animals that sleep by day and hunt for food at night.

nodding skin
A milky transparent skin covering an owl's eye that closes sideways from the base of its bill. This nodding skin allows an owl to keep its eyes moist and clean without having to shut them.

omnivore
An animal that eats both animals and plants.

order
The fourth of seven divisions in the biological classification system proposed by the Swedish botanist-naturalist Carolus Linnaeus. The order is the main subdivision of the class and contains many different families. Owls belong to the order Strigiformes.

pellet
A round ball of hair, feathers, bones, teeth, and other indigestible matter that is regurgitated by an owl.

phylum (plural: **phyla**)
The second of seven divisions in the biological classification system proposed by the Swedish botanist-naturalist Carolus Linnaeus. A phylum is one of the main divisions of a kingdom.   Owls belong to the phylum Chordata (consisting mainly of vertebrates).

sanctuary
A reservation for animals. In sanctuaries, animals are sheltered for breeding purposes and may not be hunted or otherwise molested.

spatial hearing
The ability of an owl to determine the direction and distance of a noise with precision. Spatial hearing allows the owl to hunt with its ears.

spatial sight
An owl's ability to look at an object and accurately judge its location. Because the owl's eyes are in the front of its head, it can accurately calculate distance.

species
The last of seven divisions in the biological classification system proposed by the Swedish botanist-naturalist Carolus Linnaeus. The species is the main subdivision of the genus. It may include further subgroups of its own, called subspecies. At the level of species, members share many features and are capable of breeding with one another. There are twenty-five species of owls worldwide.

MORE BOOKS ABOUT OWLS

The following books will give you more information about owls.

A First Look at Owls, Eagles, and Other Hunters of the Sky. Millicent E. Selsam and Joyce Hunt
   (Walter & Co.)
The Great Horned Owl. Lynn M. Stone (Crestwood House)
The Owl in the Tree. Jennifer Coldrey (Gareth Stevens)
Owls. John Sparks and Tony Soper (Taplinger Publishing)
Owls. Wildlife Education Ltd. Staff (Wildlife Education)
Snowy Owls. Patricia Hunt (Putnam Publishing Group)
A Year in the Life of an Owl. Alan Harris (Silver)

PLACES TO WRITE

The following are some of the many organizations that exist to educate people about animals, promote the protection of animals, and encourage the conservation of their environments. Write to these organizations for more information about owls, other animals, or animal concerns of interest to you. When you write, include your name, address, and age, and tell them clearly what you want to know. Don't forget to enclose a stamped, self-addressed envelope for a reply.

African Wildlife Foundation
1717 Massachusetts Avenue NW
Washington, D.C. 20036

Canadian Wildlife Federation
1673 Carling Avenue, Suite 203
Ottawa, Ontario K2A 3Z1

World Wildlife Fund (Canada)
90 Eglinton Avenue East, Suite 504
Toronto, Ontario M4P 2Z7

Elsa Clubs of America
P.O. Box 4572
North Hollywood, California
   91617-0572

Student Action Corps for Animals
P.O. Box 15588
Washington, D.C. 20003

World Wildlife Fund (U.S.)
1250 24th Street NW
Washington, D.C. 20037

THINGS TO DO

These projects are designed to help you have fun with what you've learned about owls. Many of them you can do alone. Some would be better to do in small groups or as class projects.

1. Now that you have read this book, spend a day at the zoo. Does the zoo have any owls? If so, can you identify them?

2. Find your home (country, state, province) on the map in this book. Do any owls make their homes in your area?

3. Carolus Linnaeus and Charles Darwin contributed greatly to the world's understanding of living things — especially animals. You might want to do further research on one of these two scientists. Using Linnaeus's system of biological classification, classify your favorite animal, listing the name of its specific group at each level.

4. Have you ever considered becoming a naturalist, a biologist, a veterinarian, or other animal-related scientist? Investigate these professions and see what training is necessary to work in these fields.

INDEX